50 Low-Carb Keto Kitchen Recipes

By: Kelly Johnson

Table of Contents

- Zucchini Noodles with Pesto
- Cauliflower Fried Rice
- Keto Chicken Alfredo
- Stuffed Bell Peppers with Ground Turkey
- Eggplant Lasagna
- Avocado and Bacon Salad
- Creamy Garlic Mushroom Chicken
- Broccoli Cheddar Soup
- Keto Meatballs in Marinara Sauce
- Shrimp and Avocado Salad
- Cheesy Cauliflower Casserole
- Chicken Thighs with Lemon and Herbs
- Spinach and Feta Stuffed Chicken Breast
- Keto Beef Stir-Fry with Vegetables
- Coconut Curry Shrimp
- Almond Flour Pancakes
- Buffalo Cauliflower Bites
- Baked Salmon with Asparagus
- Cabbage and Sausage Skillet
- Keto Egg Muffins with Veggies
- Chaffle (Cheese Waffle) Sandwich
- Roasted Brussels Sprouts with Bacon
- Pork Chops with Creamy Mushroom Sauce
- Zucchini Fritters with Sour Cream
- Keto Taco Salad
- Baked Chicken Wings with Garlic Butter
- Creamy Tuscan Garlic Chicken
- Keto Egg Salad Lettuce Wraps
- Savory Spinach and Cheese Muffins
- Ratatouille with Zucchini and Eggplant
- Greek Salad with Olives and Feta
- Beef and Broccoli Stir-Fry
- Keto Chocolate Chip Cookies
- Coconut Flour Pizza Crust
- Herb-Crusted Rack of Lamb

- Stuffed Mushrooms with Sausage
- Creamy Avocado Dressing
- Cabbage Roll Casserole
- Lemon Butter Shrimp with Zoodles
- Cauliflower Pizza Bites
- Chicken Caesar Salad
- Spaghetti Squash with Meat Sauce
- Keto Chocolate Mousse
- Almond Butter Fat Bombs
- Shrimp Scampi with Zucchini Noodles
- Bacon-Wrapped Asparagus
- Chicken Cacciatore
- Pesto Zoodle Bowl
- Keto Cheeseburger Casserole
- Creamy Pumpkin Soup

Zucchini Noodles with Pesto

Ingredients:

- 4 medium zucchini, spiralized
- 1 cup basil pesto (store-bought or homemade)
- Cherry tomatoes, halved (optional)
- Grated Parmesan cheese (optional)
- Olive oil, for cooking

Instructions:

1. **Sauté Zoodles:** In a skillet, heat a little olive oil over medium heat. Add spiralized zucchini and sauté for 2-3 minutes until just tender.
2. **Add Pesto:** Remove from heat and stir in pesto until well combined. Add cherry tomatoes if using.
3. **Serve:** Top with grated Parmesan cheese if desired and enjoy!

Cauliflower Fried Rice

Ingredients:

- 1 head cauliflower, grated or processed into rice-sized pieces
- 2 tablespoons olive oil
- 2 eggs, beaten
- 1 cup mixed vegetables (peas, carrots, bell peppers)
- 2 green onions, chopped
- Soy sauce or tamari, to taste
- Salt and pepper, to taste

Instructions:

1. **Cook Eggs:** In a large skillet, heat 1 tablespoon of olive oil over medium heat. Scramble the beaten eggs until cooked, then set aside.
2. **Sauté Veggies:** In the same skillet, add another tablespoon of olive oil. Add mixed vegetables and cook until tender.
3. **Add Cauliflower Rice:** Stir in cauliflower rice and cook for 5-7 minutes until softened. Add cooked eggs, soy sauce, salt, and pepper.
4. **Serve:** Garnish with chopped green onions and enjoy!

Keto Chicken Alfredo

Ingredients:

- 2 chicken breasts, sliced
- 1 cup heavy cream
- 1/2 cup grated Parmesan cheese
- 2 tablespoons butter
- 2 cloves garlic, minced
- Salt and pepper, to taste
- Fresh parsley, for garnish

Instructions:

1. **Cook Chicken:** In a skillet, melt butter over medium heat. Add sliced chicken and cook until golden and cooked through. Remove and set aside.
2. **Make Alfredo Sauce:** In the same skillet, add minced garlic and sauté for 1 minute. Stir in heavy cream and bring to a simmer. Whisk in Parmesan cheese until smooth. Season with salt and pepper.
3. **Combine:** Add chicken back into the skillet and coat with the sauce. Garnish with fresh parsley.
4. **Serve:** Enjoy over zucchini noodles or on its own!

Stuffed Bell Peppers with Ground Turkey

Ingredients:

- 4 bell peppers (any color)
- 1 pound ground turkey
- 1 cup cooked quinoa or cauliflower rice
- 1 can diced tomatoes (14 oz)
- 1 teaspoon Italian seasoning
- Salt and pepper, to taste
- Grated cheese (optional)

Instructions:

1. **Preheat Oven:** Preheat your oven to 375°F (190°C).
2. **Prepare Peppers:** Cut the tops off the bell peppers and remove seeds. Place in a baking dish.
3. **Cook Filling:** In a skillet, cook ground turkey until browned. Stir in quinoa or cauliflower rice, diced tomatoes, Italian seasoning, salt, and pepper.
4. **Stuff Peppers:** Fill each pepper with the turkey mixture. Top with cheese if desired.
5. **Bake:** Cover with foil and bake for 30-35 minutes until peppers are tender. Remove foil for the last 10 minutes to melt the cheese if using.
6. **Serve:** Enjoy warm!

Eggplant Lasagna

Ingredients:

- 1 large eggplant, sliced into thin rounds
- 2 cups marinara sauce
- 1 cup ricotta cheese
- 1 cup shredded mozzarella cheese
- 1/2 cup grated Parmesan cheese
- 1 teaspoon Italian seasoning
- Salt and pepper, to taste

Instructions:

1. **Preheat Oven:** Preheat your oven to 375°F (190°C).
2. **Prepare Eggplant:** Sprinkle eggplant slices with salt and let sit for 15 minutes to draw out moisture. Pat dry with a paper towel.
3. **Layer Ingredients:** In a baking dish, layer eggplant, marinara sauce, ricotta cheese, and mozzarella. Repeat layers, finishing with marinara and Parmesan cheese on top.
4. **Bake:** Cover with foil and bake for 30-40 minutes until bubbly. Remove foil for the last 10 minutes to brown the cheese.
5. **Serve:** Allow to cool slightly before slicing. Enjoy!

Avocado and Bacon Salad

Ingredients:

- 4 cups mixed greens
- 2 ripe avocados, diced
- 6 strips cooked bacon, crumbled
- 1/2 red onion, thinly sliced
- 1/4 cup cherry tomatoes, halved
- Olive oil and vinegar (for dressing)
- Salt and pepper, to taste

Instructions:

1. **Combine Ingredients:** In a large bowl, combine mixed greens, diced avocados, crumbled bacon, red onion, and cherry tomatoes.
2. **Dress Salad:** Drizzle with olive oil and vinegar, then season with salt and pepper.
3. **Toss and Serve:** Toss gently to combine and enjoy!

Creamy Garlic Mushroom Chicken

Ingredients:

- 4 chicken thighs (or breasts)
- 8 oz mushrooms, sliced
- 1 cup heavy cream
- 2 cloves garlic, minced
- 1 tablespoon olive oil
- Salt and pepper, to taste
- Fresh parsley, for garnish

Instructions:

1. **Cook Chicken:** In a skillet, heat olive oil over medium heat. Season chicken with salt and pepper and cook until golden and cooked through. Remove and set aside.
2. **Sauté Mushrooms:** In the same skillet, add mushrooms and cook until browned. Add minced garlic and sauté for another minute.
3. **Make Sauce:** Pour in heavy cream and bring to a simmer. Return chicken to the skillet and coat with the sauce.
4. **Serve:** Garnish with fresh parsley and enjoy!

Broccoli Cheddar Soup

Ingredients:

- 2 cups broccoli florets
- 1 cup shredded cheddar cheese
- 2 cups chicken or vegetable broth
- 1 cup heavy cream
- 1 small onion, diced
- 2 cloves garlic, minced
- Salt and pepper, to taste

Instructions:

1. **Sauté Onions:** In a pot, sauté diced onion in a little oil until translucent. Add garlic and cook for 1 more minute.
2. **Add Broccoli:** Add broccoli and broth. Bring to a boil, then reduce heat and simmer until broccoli is tender.
3. **Blend Soup:** Use an immersion blender or regular blender to puree the soup until smooth.
4. **Add Cream and Cheese:** Return to the pot, stir in heavy cream and cheddar cheese until melted. Season with salt and pepper.
5. **Serve:** Enjoy warm!

Keto Meatballs in Marinara Sauce

Ingredients:

- 1 pound ground beef or turkey
- 1/4 cup almond flour
- 1/4 cup grated Parmesan cheese
- 1 egg
- 2 cloves garlic, minced
- 1 teaspoon Italian seasoning
- Salt and pepper, to taste
- 2 cups marinara sauce (low-sugar)

Instructions:

1. **Preheat Oven:** Preheat your oven to 400°F (200°C).
2. **Make Meatballs:** In a bowl, combine ground meat, almond flour, Parmesan cheese, egg, garlic, Italian seasoning, salt, and pepper. Mix well and form into meatballs.
3. **Bake:** Place meatballs on a baking sheet and bake for 20-25 minutes, until cooked through.
4. **Heat Sauce:** In a skillet, heat marinara sauce. Add baked meatballs to the sauce and simmer for a few minutes.
5. **Serve:** Enjoy warm, garnished with fresh herbs if desired.

Shrimp and Avocado Salad

Ingredients:

- 1 pound shrimp, peeled and deveined
- 2 avocados, diced
- 1 cup cherry tomatoes, halved
- 1/4 cup red onion, diced
- Juice of 1 lime
- 2 tablespoons olive oil
- Salt and pepper, to taste
- Fresh cilantro (optional)

Instructions:

1. **Cook Shrimp:** In a skillet, heat olive oil over medium heat. Add shrimp and cook for 2-3 minutes on each side until pink and opaque. Season with salt and pepper.
2. **Combine Ingredients:** In a bowl, mix cooked shrimp, diced avocado, cherry tomatoes, red onion, and lime juice.
3. **Serve:** Toss gently and serve, garnished with fresh cilantro if desired.

Cheesy Cauliflower Casserole

Ingredients:

- 1 head cauliflower, cut into florets
- 1 cup shredded cheddar cheese
- 1/2 cup cream cheese, softened
- 1/2 cup sour cream
- 1/2 teaspoon garlic powder
- Salt and pepper, to taste
- 1/4 cup green onions, chopped (optional)

Instructions:

1. **Preheat Oven:** Preheat your oven to 375°F (190°C).
2. **Steam Cauliflower:** Steam cauliflower florets until tender, about 8-10 minutes. Drain and let cool slightly.
3. **Mix Casserole:** In a bowl, combine cooked cauliflower, cream cheese, sour cream, garlic powder, half of the cheddar cheese, salt, and pepper.
4. **Bake:** Transfer the mixture to a baking dish, top with remaining cheddar cheese, and bake for 25-30 minutes until bubbly and golden.
5. **Serve:** Garnish with green onions if desired and enjoy!

Chicken Thighs with Lemon and Herbs

Ingredients:

- 4 chicken thighs, bone-in and skin-on
- Juice of 1 lemon
- 2 tablespoons olive oil
- 4 cloves garlic, minced
- 1 tablespoon fresh thyme (or 1 teaspoon dried)
- Salt and pepper, to taste

Instructions:

1. **Preheat Oven:** Preheat your oven to 425°F (220°C).
2. **Marinate Chicken:** In a bowl, mix lemon juice, olive oil, garlic, thyme, salt, and pepper. Add chicken thighs and coat well. Marinate for at least 30 minutes.
3. **Bake:** Place chicken thighs in a baking dish and bake for 35-40 minutes, until cooked through and skin is crispy.
4. **Serve:** Enjoy warm with your favorite side!

Spinach and Feta Stuffed Chicken Breast

Ingredients:

- 4 boneless, skinless chicken breasts
- 2 cups fresh spinach, chopped
- 1/2 cup feta cheese, crumbled
- 1/4 cup cream cheese, softened
- 2 cloves garlic, minced
- Salt and pepper, to taste
- Olive oil, for cooking

Instructions:

1. **Preheat Oven:** Preheat your oven to 375°F (190°C).
2. **Prepare Filling:** In a bowl, mix spinach, feta cheese, cream cheese, garlic, salt, and pepper.
3. **Stuff Chicken:** Cut a pocket in each chicken breast and fill with the spinach mixture. Secure with toothpicks if needed.
4. **Sear and Bake:** In a skillet, heat olive oil over medium-high heat. Sear chicken breasts on both sides until golden, then transfer to the oven and bake for 25-30 minutes until cooked through.
5. **Serve:** Enjoy warm!

Keto Beef Stir-Fry with Vegetables

Ingredients:

- 1 pound beef (sirloin or flank steak), sliced thinly
- 2 cups mixed low-carb vegetables (broccoli, bell peppers, zucchini)
- 2 tablespoons soy sauce or coconut aminos
- 1 tablespoon sesame oil
- 2 cloves garlic, minced
- 1 teaspoon ginger, minced
- Salt and pepper, to taste
- Sesame seeds (optional, for garnish)

Instructions:

1. **Cook Beef:** In a large skillet or wok, heat sesame oil over high heat. Add beef and cook until browned, about 2-3 minutes. Remove and set aside.
2. **Sauté Vegetables:** In the same skillet, add garlic and ginger. Stir in mixed vegetables and cook until tender.
3. **Combine and Serve:** Return beef to the skillet, add soy sauce, and stir to combine. Cook for another 2 minutes. Serve warm, garnished with sesame seeds if desired.

Coconut Curry Shrimp

Ingredients:

- 1 pound shrimp, peeled and deveined
- 1 can (13.5 oz) coconut milk
- 2 tablespoons red curry paste
- 1 cup bell peppers, sliced
- 1 cup spinach
- 2 tablespoons lime juice
- Salt, to taste
- Fresh cilantro, for garnish

Instructions:

1. **Cook Vegetables:** In a pot, heat a little oil over medium heat. Add bell peppers and cook until softened.
2. **Add Curry Paste:** Stir in red curry paste and cook for another minute.
3. **Add Coconut Milk:** Pour in coconut milk and bring to a simmer. Add shrimp and cook until pink and cooked through, about 5 minutes. Stir in spinach and lime juice.
4. **Serve:** Garnish with fresh cilantro and enjoy!

Almond Flour Pancakes

Ingredients:

- 1 cup almond flour
- 2 eggs
- 1/4 cup almond milk (or any milk of choice)
- 1 teaspoon baking powder
- 1 teaspoon vanilla extract
- Pinch of salt
- Butter or oil, for cooking

Instructions:

1. **Mix Ingredients:** In a bowl, combine almond flour, baking powder, and salt. In another bowl, whisk eggs, almond milk, and vanilla extract. Combine wet and dry ingredients.
2. **Cook Pancakes:** Heat a non-stick skillet over medium heat and add butter or oil. Pour batter to form pancakes and cook until bubbles form, then flip and cook until golden.
3. **Serve:** Enjoy warm with your favorite low-carb syrup or toppings!

Buffalo Cauliflower Bites

Ingredients:

- 1 head cauliflower, cut into florets
- 1/2 cup almond flour
- 1 teaspoon garlic powder
- 1 teaspoon onion powder
- 1/2 teaspoon salt
- 1/2 cup buffalo sauce
- Olive oil spray

Instructions:

1. **Preheat Oven:** Preheat your oven to 450°F (230°C) and line a baking sheet with parchment paper.
2. **Coat Cauliflower:** In a bowl, mix almond flour, garlic powder, onion powder, and salt. Toss cauliflower florets in the mixture until well coated.
3. **Bake:** Arrange coated cauliflower on the baking sheet and spray lightly with olive oil. Bake for 20 minutes or until golden.
4. **Buffalo Sauce:** Remove from oven and toss in buffalo sauce. Return to the oven for another 10 minutes.
5. **Serve:** Enjoy warm with ranch or blue cheese dressing!

Baked Salmon with Asparagus

Ingredients:

- 4 salmon fillets
- 1 bunch asparagus, trimmed
- 2 tablespoons olive oil
- 2 cloves garlic, minced
- Juice of 1 lemon
- Salt and pepper, to taste

Instructions:

1. **Preheat Oven:** Preheat your oven to 400°F (200°C).
2. **Prepare Baking Sheet:** Arrange salmon fillets and asparagus on a baking sheet. Drizzle with olive oil and lemon juice, then sprinkle with garlic, salt, and pepper.
3. **Bake:** Bake for 12-15 minutes, or until salmon is cooked through and asparagus is tender.
4. **Serve:** Enjoy warm, garnished with lemon wedges if desired.

Cabbage and Sausage Skillet

Ingredients:

- 1 head green cabbage, chopped
- 1 pound smoked sausage or kielbasa, sliced
- 1 onion, diced
- 2 tablespoons olive oil
- Salt and pepper, to taste
- 1 teaspoon paprika (optional)

Instructions:

1. **Cook Sausage:** In a large skillet, heat olive oil over medium heat. Add sliced sausage and cook until browned.
2. **Add Onion and Cabbage:** Add diced onion and cook until translucent. Stir in chopped cabbage and season with salt, pepper, and paprika.
3. **Sauté:** Cook, stirring occasionally, until cabbage is tender, about 10-15 minutes.
4. **Serve:** Enjoy warm as a hearty meal!

Keto Egg Muffins with Veggies

Ingredients:

- 6 large eggs
- 1/2 cup bell peppers, diced
- 1/2 cup spinach, chopped
- 1/4 cup cheese (cheddar or feta)
- Salt and pepper, to taste
- Olive oil spray

Instructions:

1. **Preheat Oven:** Preheat your oven to 350°F (175°C) and spray a muffin tin with olive oil.
2. **Mix Ingredients:** In a bowl, whisk together eggs, diced bell peppers, spinach, cheese, salt, and pepper.
3. **Fill Muffin Tin:** Pour the mixture evenly into the muffin tin cups.
4. **Bake:** Bake for 20-25 minutes, or until the egg muffins are set and lightly golden.
5. **Serve:** Allow to cool slightly before removing. Enjoy warm or cold!

Chaffle (Cheese Waffle) Sandwich

Ingredients:

- 1 cup shredded cheese (cheddar or mozzarella)
- 2 large eggs
- Optional: seasonings (garlic powder, onion powder, etc.)

Instructions:

1. **Preheat Waffle Maker:** Preheat your waffle maker.
2. **Mix Ingredients:** In a bowl, combine shredded cheese and eggs. Mix until well combined.
3. **Cook Chaffles:** Pour half of the mixture into the waffle maker and cook according to the manufacturer's instructions until golden brown.
4. **Assemble Sandwich:** Use chaffles as bread for your favorite sandwich fillings, such as deli meats, avocado, or veggies.
5. **Serve:** Enjoy warm!

Roasted Brussels Sprouts with Bacon

Ingredients:

- 1 pound Brussels sprouts, halved
- 4 strips bacon, chopped
- 2 tablespoons olive oil
- Salt and pepper, to taste
- Balsamic vinegar (optional, for drizzling)

Instructions:

1. **Preheat Oven:** Preheat your oven to 400°F (200°C).
2. **Prepare Baking Sheet:** On a baking sheet, toss halved Brussels sprouts and chopped bacon with olive oil, salt, and pepper.
3. **Roast:** Roast in the oven for 20-25 minutes, or until Brussels sprouts are tender and bacon is crispy.
4. **Serve:** Drizzle with balsamic vinegar if desired and enjoy warm!

Pork Chops with Creamy Mushroom Sauce

Ingredients:

- 4 pork chops
- 1 cup mushrooms, sliced
- 1 cup heavy cream
- 2 tablespoons butter
- 2 cloves garlic, minced
- Salt and pepper, to taste
- Fresh parsley, for garnish

Instructions:

1. **Cook Pork Chops:** In a skillet, heat butter over medium heat. Season pork chops with salt and pepper, and cook until browned and cooked through, about 5-7 minutes per side. Remove and set aside.
2. **Make Sauce:** In the same skillet, add mushrooms and garlic. Sauté until mushrooms are tender. Pour in heavy cream and simmer until thickened.
3. **Combine:** Return pork chops to the skillet, coating them in the sauce.
4. **Serve:** Garnish with fresh parsley and enjoy warm!

Zucchini Fritters with Sour Cream

Ingredients:

- 2 medium zucchinis, grated
- 1/4 cup almond flour
- 2 large eggs
- 1/4 cup green onions, chopped
- Salt and pepper, to taste
- Olive oil, for frying
- Sour cream, for serving

Instructions:

1. **Prepare Zucchini:** Squeeze excess moisture from grated zucchini using a clean kitchen towel.
2. **Mix Fritter Ingredients:** In a bowl, combine zucchini, almond flour, eggs, green onions, salt, and pepper.
3. **Fry Fritters:** Heat olive oil in a skillet over medium heat. Drop spoonfuls of the mixture into the skillet and flatten slightly. Cook until golden brown on both sides.
4. **Serve:** Enjoy warm with a dollop of sour cream!

Keto Taco Salad

Ingredients:

- 1 pound ground beef
- 1 tablespoon taco seasoning (or to taste)
- 4 cups romaine lettuce, chopped
- 1 cup cherry tomatoes, halved
- 1/2 cup cheddar cheese, shredded
- 1/4 cup sour cream
- 1/4 cup salsa (low-sugar)
- 1 avocado, diced
- Olive oil (optional, for drizzling)

Instructions:

1. **Cook Beef:** In a skillet over medium heat, brown the ground beef. Add taco seasoning and cook according to package instructions. Set aside.
2. **Assemble Salad:** In a large bowl, combine chopped lettuce, cherry tomatoes, cheese, avocado, and cooked beef.
3. **Dress Salad:** Top with sour cream and salsa. Drizzle with olive oil if desired.
4. **Serve:** Toss gently and enjoy!

Baked Chicken Wings with Garlic Butter

Ingredients:

- 2 pounds chicken wings
- 1/4 cup butter, melted
- 4 cloves garlic, minced
- 1 teaspoon paprika
- Salt and pepper, to taste
- Fresh parsley, for garnish

Instructions:

1. **Preheat Oven:** Preheat your oven to 400°F (200°C) and line a baking sheet with parchment paper.
2. **Prepare Wings:** In a bowl, mix melted butter, garlic, paprika, salt, and pepper. Toss chicken wings in the mixture until well coated.
3. **Bake Wings:** Arrange wings on the baking sheet and bake for 40-45 minutes, turning halfway, until crispy.
4. **Serve:** Garnish with fresh parsley and enjoy warm!

Creamy Tuscan Garlic Chicken

Ingredients:

- 4 boneless, skinless chicken breasts
- 2 tablespoons olive oil
- 3 cloves garlic, minced
- 1 cup heavy cream
- 1 cup spinach, chopped
- 1/2 cup sun-dried tomatoes, chopped
- 1 teaspoon Italian seasoning
- Salt and pepper, to taste

Instructions:

1. **Cook Chicken:** In a skillet, heat olive oil over medium heat. Season chicken breasts with salt and pepper, then cook until golden brown and cooked through, about 6-7 minutes per side. Remove and set aside.
2. **Make Sauce:** In the same skillet, add garlic and sauté until fragrant. Pour in heavy cream, then add spinach, sun-dried tomatoes, Italian seasoning, salt, and pepper. Simmer for a few minutes until slightly thickened.
3. **Combine:** Return chicken to the skillet, coating it in the sauce.
4. **Serve:** Enjoy warm, garnished with fresh herbs if desired!

Keto Egg Salad Lettuce Wraps

Ingredients:

- 6 hard-boiled eggs, chopped
- 1/4 cup mayonnaise (or to taste)
- 1 teaspoon mustard
- Salt and pepper, to taste
- 1 tablespoon green onions, chopped
- Butter lettuce leaves for wrapping

Instructions:

1. **Mix Egg Salad:** In a bowl, combine chopped eggs, mayonnaise, mustard, salt, pepper, and green onions. Mix well.
2. **Assemble Wraps:** Spoon egg salad onto lettuce leaves and wrap them up.
3. **Serve:** Enjoy as a light lunch or snack!

Savory Spinach and Cheese Muffins

Ingredients:

- 2 cups almond flour
- 4 large eggs
- 1 cup fresh spinach, chopped
- 1/2 cup cheese (cheddar or feta), shredded
- 1 teaspoon baking powder
- Salt and pepper, to taste

Instructions:

1. **Preheat Oven:** Preheat your oven to 350°F (175°C) and grease a muffin tin.
2. **Mix Ingredients:** In a bowl, combine almond flour, baking powder, eggs, spinach, cheese, salt, and pepper. Mix until well combined.
3. **Fill Muffin Tin:** Spoon the mixture into the muffin tin, filling each cup about 3/4 full.
4. **Bake:** Bake for 20-25 minutes or until golden brown and a toothpick comes out clean.
5. **Serve:** Enjoy warm or store for later!

Ratatouille with Zucchini and Eggplant

Ingredients:

- 1 eggplant, diced
- 2 zucchinis, sliced
- 1 bell pepper, diced
- 1 onion, diced
- 2 cups tomatoes, chopped (or 1 can diced tomatoes)
- 3 cloves garlic, minced
- 2 tablespoons olive oil
- 1 teaspoon Italian seasoning
- Salt and pepper, to taste

Instructions:

1. **Sauté Vegetables:** In a large skillet, heat olive oil over medium heat. Add onion and garlic, sautéing until translucent.
2. **Add Veggies:** Stir in eggplant, zucchini, and bell pepper. Cook for 5-7 minutes until tender.
3. **Simmer:** Add tomatoes, Italian seasoning, salt, and pepper. Simmer for 15-20 minutes, stirring occasionally.
4. **Serve:** Enjoy warm as a side dish or main course!

Greek Salad with Olives and Feta

Ingredients:

- 2 cups cucumber, diced
- 1 cup cherry tomatoes, halved
- 1/2 cup red onion, thinly sliced
- 1/2 cup olives (Kalamata or green)
- 1/2 cup feta cheese, crumbled
- 2 tablespoons olive oil
- 1 tablespoon red wine vinegar
- Salt and pepper, to taste

Instructions:

1. **Combine Ingredients:** In a large bowl, combine cucumber, cherry tomatoes, red onion, olives, and feta cheese.
2. **Dress Salad:** Drizzle with olive oil and red wine vinegar. Season with salt and pepper.
3. **Toss and Serve:** Toss gently and enjoy fresh!

Beef and Broccoli Stir-Fry

Ingredients:

- 1 pound beef (flank or sirloin), sliced thinly
- 2 cups broccoli florets
- 2 tablespoons soy sauce or coconut aminos
- 2 tablespoons olive oil
- 2 cloves garlic, minced
- 1 teaspoon ginger, minced
- Salt and pepper, to taste

Instructions:

1. **Cook Beef:** In a large skillet, heat olive oil over medium-high heat. Add sliced beef and cook until browned. Remove and set aside.
2. **Sauté Broccoli:** In the same skillet, add garlic and ginger, then stir in broccoli. Cook until tender-crisp, about 3-5 minutes.
3. **Combine and Serve:** Return beef to the skillet, add soy sauce, and stir to combine. Cook for another 2 minutes, then serve warm!

Keto Chocolate Chip Cookies

Ingredients:

- 1 cup almond flour
- 1/2 cup coconut flour
- 1/2 cup butter, softened
- 1/2 cup erythritol (or preferred sweetener)
- 1 large egg
- 1 teaspoon vanilla extract
- 1/2 teaspoon baking soda
- 1/4 teaspoon salt
- 1/2 cup sugar-free chocolate chips

Instructions:

1. **Preheat Oven:** Preheat your oven to 350°F (175°C) and line a baking sheet with parchment paper.
2. **Mix Ingredients:** In a bowl, cream together butter and erythritol. Add the egg and vanilla, mixing until smooth. Stir in almond flour, coconut flour, baking soda, and salt until well combined. Fold in chocolate chips.
3. **Form Cookies:** Scoop tablespoon-sized balls of dough onto the baking sheet, spacing them apart.
4. **Bake:** Bake for 10-12 minutes, until golden. Let cool before serving.

Coconut Flour Pizza Crust

Ingredients:

- 1 cup coconut flour
- 1/2 cup shredded mozzarella cheese
- 2 large eggs
- 1/4 cup olive oil
- 1 teaspoon baking powder
- 1 teaspoon Italian seasoning
- Salt, to taste

Instructions:

1. **Preheat Oven:** Preheat your oven to 400°F (200°C) and line a baking sheet with parchment paper.
2. **Mix Ingredients:** In a bowl, combine coconut flour, mozzarella cheese, eggs, olive oil, baking powder, Italian seasoning, and salt. Mix until a dough forms.
3. **Shape Crust:** Spread the dough on the prepared baking sheet into your desired pizza shape.
4. **Bake:** Bake for 15-20 minutes until golden brown. Add your favorite keto toppings and bake again until heated through.

Herb-Crusted Rack of Lamb

Ingredients:

- 1 rack of lamb, frenched
- 2 tablespoons olive oil
- 1 tablespoon Dijon mustard
- 1/2 cup fresh herbs (rosemary, thyme, parsley), chopped
- Salt and pepper, to taste

Instructions:

1. **Preheat Oven:** Preheat your oven to 400°F (200°C).
2. **Prepare Lamb:** Rub the rack of lamb with olive oil and Dijon mustard. Season with salt and pepper. Coat with the chopped herbs.
3. **Roast:** Place the lamb on a roasting pan and roast for 20-25 minutes for medium-rare. Let rest before slicing.
4. **Serve:** Enjoy with your favorite low-carb sides!

Stuffed Mushrooms with Sausage

Ingredients:

- 1 pound large mushrooms, stems removed
- 1 pound Italian sausage, cooked and crumbled
- 1/2 cup cream cheese, softened
- 1/4 cup parmesan cheese, grated
- 2 tablespoons fresh parsley, chopped
- Salt and pepper, to taste

Instructions:

1. **Preheat Oven:** Preheat your oven to 375°F (190°C).
2. **Mix Filling:** In a bowl, combine cooked sausage, cream cheese, parmesan cheese, parsley, salt, and pepper.
3. **Stuff Mushrooms:** Fill each mushroom cap with the sausage mixture.
4. **Bake:** Arrange on a baking sheet and bake for 20-25 minutes until mushrooms are tender.
5. **Serve:** Enjoy warm as an appetizer!

Creamy Avocado Dressing

Ingredients:

- 1 ripe avocado
- 1/2 cup Greek yogurt
- 1 tablespoon lemon juice
- 1 clove garlic, minced
- Salt and pepper, to taste
- Water, to thin (optional)

Instructions:

1. **Blend Ingredients:** In a blender, combine avocado, Greek yogurt, lemon juice, garlic, salt, and pepper. Blend until smooth.
2. **Adjust Consistency:** If the dressing is too thick, add water a tablespoon at a time until desired consistency is reached.
3. **Serve:** Use as a dressing for salads or a dip for veggies!

Cabbage Roll Casserole

Ingredients:

- 1 head cabbage, chopped
- 1 pound ground beef or turkey
- 1 can diced tomatoes (14 oz)
- 1 cup cauliflower rice
- 1 onion, diced
- 1 teaspoon garlic powder
- Salt and pepper, to taste
- 1 tablespoon Italian seasoning

Instructions:

1. **Preheat Oven:** Preheat your oven to 375°F (190°C).
2. **Sauté Cabbage:** In a large skillet, sauté chopped cabbage and onion until softened.
3. **Mix Filling:** In a bowl, combine ground meat, diced tomatoes, cauliflower rice, garlic powder, salt, pepper, and Italian seasoning.
4. **Layer Casserole:** In a baking dish, layer half of the cabbage, followed by the meat mixture, and then the remaining cabbage.
5. **Bake:** Cover and bake for 30-35 minutes until cooked through. Let cool slightly before serving.

Lemon Butter Shrimp with Zoodles

Ingredients:

- 1 pound shrimp, peeled and deveined
- 2 medium zucchini, spiralized
- 4 tablespoons butter
- 2 cloves garlic, minced
- Juice of 1 lemon
- Salt and pepper, to taste
- Fresh parsley, for garnish

Instructions:

1. **Sauté Shrimp:** In a skillet, melt butter over medium heat. Add garlic and sauté until fragrant. Add shrimp, season with salt and pepper, and cook until pink and cooked through.
2. **Add Zoodles:** Add spiralized zucchini to the skillet, tossing to combine. Cook for 2-3 minutes until zoodles are tender.
3. **Finish with Lemon:** Squeeze lemon juice over the dish and garnish with fresh parsley.
4. **Serve:** Enjoy warm!

Cauliflower Pizza Bites

Ingredients:

- 2 cups cauliflower rice (fresh or frozen)
- 1 cup shredded mozzarella cheese
- 1/4 cup almond flour
- 1 large egg
- 1 teaspoon Italian seasoning
- Salt and pepper, to taste

Instructions:

1. **Preheat Oven:** Preheat your oven to 400°F (200°C) and line a baking sheet with parchment paper.
2. **Mix Ingredients:** In a bowl, combine cauliflower rice, mozzarella cheese, almond flour, egg, Italian seasoning, salt, and pepper.
3. **Form Bites:** Scoop the mixture and form small bites, placing them on the prepared baking sheet.
4. **Bake:** Bake for 15-20 minutes until golden brown. Serve with marinara sauce for dipping!

Chicken Caesar Salad

Ingredients:

- 2 cups romaine lettuce, chopped
- 1 cup cooked chicken, sliced
- 1/4 cup parmesan cheese, grated
- 1/4 cup Caesar dressing (low-carb)
- Croutons (optional, or use crushed pork rinds)

Instructions:

1. **Assemble Salad:** In a large bowl, combine chopped romaine, sliced chicken, and parmesan cheese.
2. **Dress Salad:** Drizzle with Caesar dressing and toss to coat.
3. **Serve:** Top with croutons or crushed pork rinds if desired and enjoy!

Spaghetti Squash with Meat Sauce

Ingredients:

- 1 medium spaghetti squash
- 1 pound ground beef or turkey
- 1 can (14 oz) crushed tomatoes
- 1 onion, diced
- 2 cloves garlic, minced
- 1 teaspoon Italian seasoning
- Salt and pepper, to taste
- Olive oil

Instructions:

1. **Prepare Squash:** Preheat the oven to 400°F (200°C). Cut the spaghetti squash in half lengthwise, remove seeds, and brush with olive oil. Place cut side down on a baking sheet. Bake for 30-40 minutes until tender.
2. **Cook Meat Sauce:** In a skillet, heat olive oil over medium heat. Sauté onion and garlic until translucent. Add ground meat, cooking until browned. Stir in crushed tomatoes, Italian seasoning, salt, and pepper. Simmer for 10-15 minutes.
3. **Serve:** Scrape the flesh of the squash with a fork to create "noodles." Top with meat sauce and enjoy!

Keto Chocolate Mousse

Ingredients:

- 1 cup heavy cream
- 1/4 cup unsweetened cocoa powder
- 1/4 cup erythritol (or preferred sweetener)
- 1 teaspoon vanilla extract

Instructions:

1. **Whip Cream:** In a bowl, whip the heavy cream until soft peaks form.
2. **Add Ingredients:** Gently fold in cocoa powder, erythritol, and vanilla until well combined.
3. **Chill and Serve:** Spoon into serving dishes and refrigerate for at least 30 minutes before serving.

Almond Butter Fat Bombs

Ingredients:

- 1/2 cup almond butter
- 1/4 cup coconut oil, melted
- 2 tablespoons erythritol (or preferred sweetener)
- 1 teaspoon vanilla extract
- A pinch of salt

Instructions:

1. **Mix Ingredients:** In a bowl, combine almond butter, melted coconut oil, erythritol, vanilla, and salt. Mix until smooth.
2. **Mold Fat Bombs:** Pour the mixture into silicone molds or an ice cube tray. Freeze for at least 30 minutes until solid.
3. **Serve:** Pop out the fat bombs and store in the fridge or freezer.

Shrimp Scampi with Zucchini Noodles

Ingredients:

- 1 pound shrimp, peeled and deveined
- 2 medium zucchini, spiralized
- 4 tablespoons butter
- 3 cloves garlic, minced
- Juice of 1 lemon
- Salt and pepper, to taste
- Fresh parsley, for garnish

Instructions:

1. **Cook Shrimp:** In a skillet, melt butter over medium heat. Add garlic and sauté until fragrant. Add shrimp, cooking until pink and opaque.
2. **Add Zoodles:** Add spiralized zucchini to the skillet, tossing to combine. Cook for 2-3 minutes until zucchini is tender.
3. **Finish with Lemon:** Squeeze lemon juice over the dish and garnish with parsley before serving.

Bacon-Wrapped Asparagus

Ingredients:

- 1 bunch asparagus, trimmed
- 8 slices bacon
- Olive oil
- Salt and pepper, to taste

Instructions:

1. **Preheat Oven:** Preheat your oven to 400°F (200°C).
2. **Wrap Asparagus:** Take one slice of bacon and wrap it around each asparagus spear, securing it with a toothpick if necessary.
3. **Bake:** Place on a baking sheet, drizzle with olive oil, and season with salt and pepper. Bake for 15-20 minutes until bacon is crispy.

Chicken Cacciatore

Ingredients:

- 1 pound chicken thighs, skin-on
- 1 can (14 oz) diced tomatoes
- 1 bell pepper, sliced
- 1 onion, sliced
- 2 cloves garlic, minced
- 1 teaspoon Italian seasoning
- Salt and pepper, to taste
- Olive oil

Instructions:

1. **Sear Chicken:** In a large skillet, heat olive oil over medium heat. Season chicken with salt and pepper, then sear until browned on both sides. Remove and set aside.
2. **Sauté Veggies:** In the same skillet, sauté onion, garlic, and bell pepper until soft. Add diced tomatoes and Italian seasoning.
3. **Simmer:** Return chicken to the skillet, cover, and simmer for 30-40 minutes until chicken is cooked through.

Pesto Zoodle Bowl

Ingredients:

- 2 medium zucchini, spiralized
- 1/2 cup basil pesto (store-bought or homemade)
- 1 cup cherry tomatoes, halved
- 1/4 cup pine nuts (optional)
- Grated Parmesan cheese, for serving

Instructions:

1. **Cook Zoodles:** In a skillet, lightly sauté zucchini noodles for 2-3 minutes until just tender.
2. **Mix with Pesto:** Remove from heat and toss with pesto and cherry tomatoes.
3. **Serve:** Top with pine nuts and grated Parmesan before serving.

Keto Cheeseburger Casserole

Ingredients:

- 1 pound ground beef
- 1/2 cup onion, diced
- 2 cups cauliflower rice
- 1 cup shredded cheddar cheese
- 4 large eggs
- 1/2 cup heavy cream
- 1 tablespoon mustard
- Salt and pepper, to taste

Instructions:

1. **Preheat Oven:** Preheat your oven to 350°F (175°C).
2. **Cook Beef:** In a skillet, cook ground beef and onion until browned. Drain excess fat.
3. **Mix Ingredients:** In a bowl, whisk together eggs, heavy cream, mustard, salt, and pepper. Combine with cooked beef and cauliflower rice. Pour into a greased baking dish.
4. **Bake:** Top with cheese and bake for 25-30 minutes until set and golden.

Creamy Pumpkin Soup

Ingredients:

- 1 can (15 oz) pumpkin puree
- 2 cups chicken or vegetable broth
- 1 cup heavy cream
- 1 teaspoon pumpkin pie spice
- Salt and pepper, to taste

Instructions:

1. **Combine Ingredients:** In a pot, combine pumpkin puree, broth, heavy cream, pumpkin pie spice, salt, and pepper. Stir well.
2. **Heat:** Bring to a simmer over medium heat, stirring occasionally.
3. **Serve:** Once heated through, serve warm, garnished with a drizzle of cream if desired.

www.ingramcontent.com/pod-product-compliance
Lightning Source LLC
LaVergne TN
LVHW081341060526
838201LV00055B/2782